Heart of Oak

HEART OF OAK

A PICTORIAL HISTORY OF THE ROYAL CANADIAN NAVY

TEXT BY J.A. FOSTER

METHUEN

Toronto   New York   London   Sydney   Auckland

**Canadian Cataloguing in Publication
Data**

Foster, Tony, 1932–
 Heart of oak

ISBN 0-458-99230-5

1. Canada. Royal Canadian Navy—
History.
I. Title.

FC231.F67 1985   359'.00971
C85-098218-9
F1028.5.F67 1985

Front cover: Captains hat badge,
circa WWII, courtesy of Frank
Stockwell.
Photograph by Philip Gallard.

Back cover: HMCS *Algonquin*,
courtesy Department of National
Defence.

Design: Jonathan Eby

Printed and bound in Canada

1 2 3 4   85   89 88 87 86

Dedicated to the tens of thousands of
men and women who served with the
Royal Canadian Navy in peacetime and
through three wars.

With acknowledgement and thanks to Marilyn G.
Smith, Curator, Maritime Command Museum, Halifax,
and Tony Melski, Porter's Lake, Nova Scotia, for their
splendid research and assistance.

CONTENTS

FOREWORD

In 1985 Canadians celebrate the seventy-fifth anniversary of their navy. A very useful and interesting contribution to the observances is the publication of this pictorial history, *Heart of Oak*.

The work, by J. A. Foster, of compiling a photographic history of the navy's first seventy-five years will be gratefully acknowledged and applauded by sailors all across the country. It provides a bookshelf reference for all who have an interest in the sea, and particularly for those men and women who have a link with the Royal Canadian Navy, the Marine Division of the Royal Canadian Mounted Police, the Merchant Marine and, later, the Sea Component of the Canadian Armed Forces.

The collection of photographs indicates the changes in warship design over the period of the history, 1910 to 1985. It will remind the viewer that life at sea in small ships is rarely free from physical hardship and, in the stormy waters of the North Atlantic, danger.

The pictures do not draw attention to the many years of neglect of the navy between the wars. At times, this negligence was so drastic that the navy all but disappeared. Yet, in times of peril the sea forces were restored and manned as quickly as ships could be built and personnel trained, a luxury in elapsed time that we may not be able to enjoy in future emergencies. It will be another five years before the new ships of the small replacement program now begun will be in place. By then all the present fleet will be fit for scrap only. The burden of defence to insure the peace we now have is very costly. For far too long Canada has not provided a fair share of the forces needed to take a reasonable place alongside our friends and allies. *Heart of Oak* shows the drama of wars, but cannot portray the ugly story of weakness that invites war.

I hope this pictorial history will remind Canadians that we enjoy the blessings of a land that provides an abundance of the necessities of life far in excess of the basic needs lacking in so many parts of the world. We take for granted the freedoms we enjoy. Surely we ought to expect adequate preparation in peace to maintain those freedoms and prevent the horrors of war.

This story begins in the first year of the reign of King George V. In 1910 Canadian sailors wore cap tallies bearing the HMCS for the first time. This was to continue through the years of King Edward VIII and King George VI and well into the reign of our present sovereign. In 1967 the Royal Canadian Navy had been renamed the Sea Component of the Canadian Armed Forces, and even the designation of "navy" was removed. These blunders will not be shown by the photos, but they are there as a part of the history, nonetheless.

These pages are naval memoirs of two world wars and the Korean conflict when Canada heeded the bidding of the United Nations. The ships are all HMCS ships, proud ships, proud to serve their sovereign and their country. They are ships proud to discharge their commitment, so well expressed in the Naval Prayer, "that we may be a safeguard unto our most gracious Sovereign Lady, Queen Elizabeth, and her Commonwealth, and a security for such as pass on the seas upon their lawful occasions."

So now read on, look on, and if you have a moment to spare, join me in a toast to the Royal Canadian Navy, the Royal Canadian Naval Reserve, the Royal Canadian Naval Volunteer Reserve and the Women's Royal Canadian Naval Service for their part in the first seventy-five years of naval service to Canada.

W. M. LANDYMORE
Rear Admiral RCN (ret.)

THE BEGINNING AND WORLD WAR I

*"It is upon the Navy, under the good
Providence of God, that the wealth, safety and
strength of the Kingdom depend."*
– BRITISH NAVAL DISCIPLINE ACT, 1866

Throughout the eighteenth and nineteenth centuries the Royal Navy ruled the sea lanes of the world. Its ships were everywhere, insuring safe passage of Britain's commerce. Canada, Australia, New Zealand, India and every British possession around the globe enjoyed the luxury of Royal Navy protection. But by 1900 this domination of the oceans was being challenged by Germany through the unbridled ambitions of her kaiser. Britain needed her navy in home waters to contain the German threat. There simply were not enough ships to go around. Britain turned to her colonies for help in solving the problem.

A Canadian financial contribution was out of the question. Proud of her new Dominion status from the mother country, Canada announced that it would establish its own navy and cooperate with Britain so far as was consistent with any self-governing nation. Brave words!

An order was placed with Vickers Son & Maxim shipyards at Barrow-in-Furness, England, for a protective cruiser to be named *Canada*. The vessel, commissioned in 1904, was designed for the Fishery Protection Service to operate along the east coast of Nova Scotia and in the Gulf of St. Lawrence. It mounted two 12-pounder QF guns, displaced 750 tons, had a speed of 17.5 knots flat out and a complement of five officers and forty-five other ranks. In October 1909, the country's first naval cadets were assigned to the *Canada* for training.

The British relinquished official control of their naval stations at Halifax and Esquimalt in the summer of 1904. By the following February the flagship of the Pacific squadron had departed for the China station. The Atlantic squadron had left the previous year.

On the east coast, the British had left one steam torpedo boat and three small harbour vessels to assist in provisioning and coaling operations when its naval ships called in Halifax. Two Royal Navy vessels remained on the west coast: HMS *Shearwater* and the surveying ship *Egeria*. In matters of naval defence for one of the world's longest coastlines, Canada was now on its own.

After a long, acrimonious debate that divided the country's political parties, the government passed the Naval Services Act on May 4, 1910, creating a Department of Naval Services under the Minister of Marine and Fisheries. The act provided for ships, a naval reserve force, a naval volunteer force and a naval college. Finally, Britain's Naval Discipline Act would be applied to the new "Royal Canadian Navy." On paper it all looked good. Reality was another matter entirely.

For political reasons, the prime minister of the day, Sir Wilfrid Laurier, decided on a modest beginning. Two aging coal-fired cruisers were purchased from Britain for training purposes: *Niobi*, based in Halifax, and *Rainbow*, operating on the west coast.

Niobi, the largest at 11,000 tons, sailed into

Halifax harbour with a skeleton crew on October 21, 1910—Trafalgar Day. Plans called for manning the vessel with raw recruits—a sort of early day learn-as-you-work program of the type that had been operating on the *Canada* over the previous year. Unfortunately, the idea never came to fruition. A combination of government indecision and continual political controversy over expenses made it very difficult to attract recruits.

More embarrassing than the government's uncertainty about the new navy was the number of desertions. Men got fed up and returned home. Between 1911 and 1912 only 112 enlistments were recorded against 149 desertions. Not a spectacular beginning for a world-class sea power. To make matters worse, *Niobi* ran aground during an early training cruise and was put out of commission for over a year while the government squabbled over the cost of repairs.

When the second cruiser, *Rainbow*, arrived at Esquimalt in 1910, HMS *Shearwater* was still there. The Royal Navy had left two ships behind—HMS *Algernine* was the other—to fulfil certain commitments by the British Admiralty in supervising the eastern Pacific sealing fleets. *Rainbow* took up duties as a training patrol ship covering coastal waters on the lookout for foreign poachers.

To overcome the shortage of vessels needed for wartime patrol work, fishing craft, small merchant vessels and other ships belonging to the government were placed in service. But the supply of suitable craft was limited. However, in the United States, numbers of steam yachts lay idle, their cruising curtailed by the war at sea. Since neutrality laws prevented the export of any vessel intended for use as a warship, the Canadian government had to figure out a method of circumventing the law. Accordingly, Canadian yachtsmen were provided with funds and sent off to purchase whatever they could find that would do the job.

J. K. Ross, Lieutenant RCNVR, visited New York in 1914 and bought the yacht *Winchester*. It was renamed HMCS *Grilse*. Built in 1912 at Glasgow on torpedo boat destroyer lines, she arrived in Halifax under Ross's command for wartime conversion and, with tongue in cheek, was formally presented as a "gift" from Ross to the Canadian government.

HMCS *Grilse* and *Tuna* were the only torpedo boats operated by Canada in the First World War. *Grilse* was equipped with two 12-pounder guns and a torpedo, but never battled anything worse than Atlantic storms throughout the war.

On December 11, 1916, she sailed from Halifax for Bermuda. Next day a message was received that she was heading for shelter at Shelburne, Nova Scotia, to escape bad weather. Later the same day an SOS came in from *Grilse*, followed a half hour later by the words "now sinking." Search vessels were sent to her aid. On December 14, the Minister of Naval Service announced her loss with all hands—fifty-six officers and men.

But just before midnight of the same day she limped into Shelburne harbour, barely recognizable but still floating. She had fought her way through 150 miles of stormy seas. Six crewmen were washed overboard. *Grilse* was brought to Halifax for repair and spent the rest of the war on Atlantic patrol.

Shearwater and *Canada* also became HMCS ships at the outbreak of war. *Shearwater* was the tender for Canada's first two submarines, *CC1* and *CC2*. She served on the west coast until 1917 when, along with her two submarines, she became the first warship flying the white ensign of the RCN to sail

HMS *Cormorant*, the first vessel docked in Esquimalt Graving Dock (Naden) June 20, 1887, before the formation of the RCN in 1910.
(Maritime Command Museum, Halifax)

△ HMS *Shearwater* with HMS *Rainbow* behind, Esquimalt, 1910. (Maritime Command Museum)   ▽ HMCS *Shearwater*. (Canadian Forces photograph/E-42424)

Crewman of HMCS *Shearwater*. (Maritime Museum of British Columbia)

Above: Torpedo boats in Halifax harbour, about 1903.
(Halifax Defence Complex, Parks Canada)

Left: HMCS *Grilse*, the first of that name.
(Department of National Defence/CN-6149)

Patrol craft at Halifax during World War I. *Left:* HMCS *Givenchy*, trawler; *right:* HMCS *Cartier*, patrol vessel. *Cartier* was built in 1910 for the Department of Marine and Fisheries as a hydrographic surveying vessel and taken up for naval service in 1917.
(Canadian Forces photograph/CN-2902)

HMCS *Niobe*.
(Canadian Forces photograph/DB-4171)

HMCS *Niobe* in drydock.
(Canadian Forces photograph/CN-6593)

△ HMCS *Niobe* gun room officers, 1910. (Maritime Museum of the Atlantic)   ▽ HMCS *Niobe* Stokers of the Watch, 1911. (Maritime Museum of the Atlantic)

△ HMCS *Canada*. (Canadian Forces photograph/CN-3793)　　　▽ Gun drill on HMCS *Canada*. (Maritime Command Museum)

The crew of HMCS *Canada*, Canada's first warship. (Maritime Command Museum, Halifax)

△ *CC1.* (Maritime Museum of British Columbia)

∇ CC2. (NDHQ)

CC Class submarine control room looking forward. Hydroplane operating handwheels on the left, helm in the centre beyond the conning tower ladder. To the right are the Kingston valve hand-levers. To the left of the helm is the high-pressure air distribution panel. The main ballast tank blowing manifold appears to the right of the bulkhead door.
(Maritime Museum of British Columbia)

At left: CC1 and *CC2* in the Panama Canal locks, August 1917.
(Maritime Museum of British Columbia)

Above left: Lieutenant Adrian Keyes and crew of *CC1* and *CC2* after first successful dive.
(Canadian Forces photograph/PMR-84-480)

Above right: Crewman of *CC1.*
(Maritime Museum of British Columbia)

Below left: Submarine crewmen.
(Maritime Museum of British Columbia)

BETWEEN THE WARS

The Canadian government of 1920 still had no postwar naval policy. This was not surprising since Britain hadn't developed one either. The whole question of naval defence for the Empire was scheduled for discussion at an upcoming Imperial Conference. Canada claimed heavy financial commitments at the conference, in the end adopting a line of least resistance—and expense—by accepting a British offer of one light cruiser, two torpedo boat destroyers and two submarines. The three ships arrived in Halifax on December 21, 1920. They weren't much of a Christmas present.

HMCS *Aurora*, the cruiser, burned oil at an alarming rate even when operating at low speeds. In addition, its maintenance costs under existing naval allocations were prohibitive. The Royal Navy was fortunate to be rid of it. The Canadian general election of 1921 solved the problem. A new Liberal government reduced the navy's budget by $1 million, leaving Captain Walter Hose, Director of Naval Services, with only $1.5 million to operate the navy.

Captain Hose decided that by disposing of *Aurora* and keeping the two torpedo boat destroyers, *Patriot* and *Patrician*, he could manage to make ends meet. But more importantly, in his view, he could create a naval reserve and volunteer reserves. With

HMCS *Aurora*, with HMCS *Patriot* and HMCS *Patrician*. (Canadian Forces photograph/CN-6546-2)

reserves distributed across the country, all Canadians would be conscious of the navy and for the first time would be able to participate in much the same way as the members of the army's active militia.

Aurora accordingly was sacrificed and paid off on July 1, 1922. The two subs, *CH 14* and *CH 15*, were paid off at the same time after scarcely being used. Five years later they were sold for scrap. With the savings realized, Hose was able to open two new shore-based establishments: HMCS *Stadacona* in Halifax and *Naden* on the Pacific coast.

For the next five years, *Patriot* and *Patrician* were the only two fully commissioned ships in the RCN. Throughout July and August 1922, they visited most of the east coast seaports. Then, in October, *Patrician* took up station on the west coast. *Patriot* remained on the east coast occupied with training exercises for her crew, nearly half of whom were untrained seamen.

In October 1922, *Patriot* towed the original fishing schooner *Bluenose* to Gloucester, Massachusetts, where the soon-to-be-famous fishing boat competed in the International Schooner Race. *Patriot* was also used in assisting Dr. Alexander Graham Bell and Casey Baldwin in their hydrofoil experiments in the Bras d'Or lakes of Nova Scotia.

Both *Patriot* and *Patrician* continued serving as training vessels for reserve personnel until 1926. Worn out, both were decommissioned in December 1927.

To replace them, HMCS *Saguenay* and *Skeena* were launched in 1930. These were the first men-of-war built for the Canadian government. These ships had lengthy and active careers and performed heroically during World War II.

Saguenay made the first east–west Atlantic crossing by a Canadian destroyer in 1936. At the unveiling of the Canadian War Memorial at Vimy Ridge on July 26, men of the *Saguenay* became the first Royal Guard ever paraded by the RCN for a reigning monarch when King Edward VIII received their salute. *Saguenay* joined the mid-ocean escort force based in St. John's, Newfoundland, in June 1941, after duty with the British Home Fleet. Her most memorable convoy assignment was at Placentia Bay with the Royal Navy battleship *Prince of Wales* when Prime Minister Churchill and his staff sailed for home after the Atlantic Conference with President Roosevelt. Later, at sea in January 1942, she ran into a hurricane with 80-foot waves that rolled the ship 60°. Frames and plates buckled under the pounding, but she managed to survive and reach St. John's for repairs. Three months later she was back at sea. She became a familiar sight on the "Derry–Newfie" convoy run, easily identifiable by her scarred hull and brightly marked funnel that distinguished her as one of the early members of the famous "Barber Pole Brigade." She was known affectionately as "Old Sag." For a while, she swung at anchor in the Annapolis Basin of Nova Scotia as tender to HMCS *Cornwallis*. New recruits received their first taste of navy life on board *Saguenay*. At war's end she was paid off with considerable nostalgia by the men who had served aboard this brave ship.

Skeena was commissioned on June 10, 1931, at Portsmouth and arrived at Halifax with *Saguenay* three weeks later. *Skeena*

Submarines, *CH14* and *CH15*.
(Canadian Forces photograph/PMR-78-517)

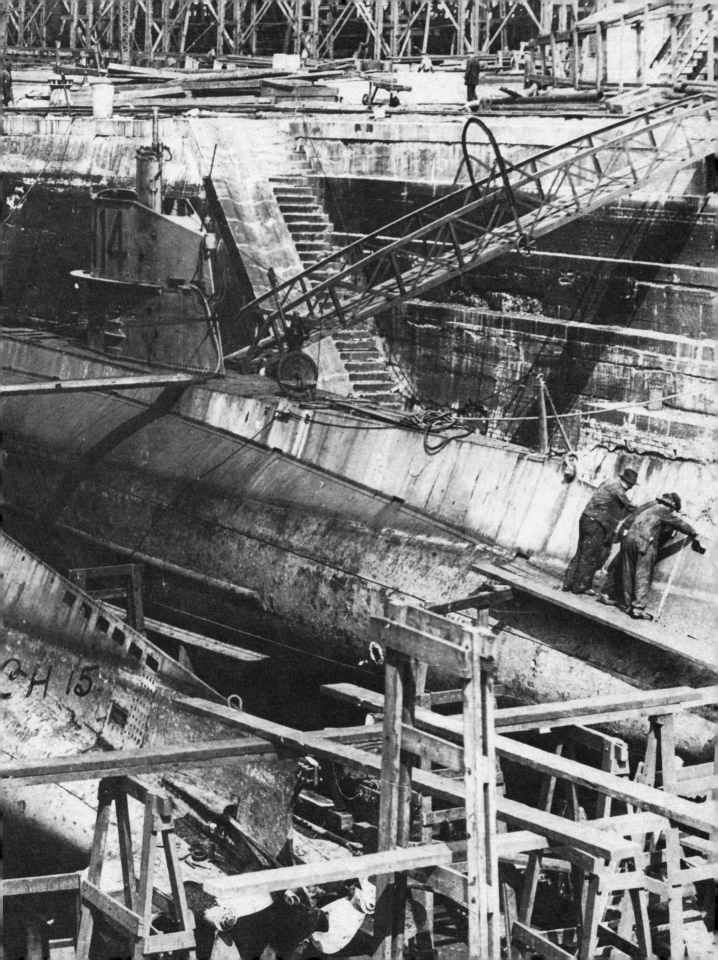

sailed on to the west coast where she remained until 1937 when she returned to Halifax. *Skeena* performed local escort duties at the outbreak of World War II. She was transferred to England in 1940 and was assigned to the Western Approaches Command. She took part in the evacuation of France and convoy escort in British waters. After a refit in Halifax in 1941, she joined the Mid-Ocean Escort Force (MOEF) under the Newfoundland Command. On July 31, 1942, while escorting convoy *ON 115*, she shared credit for sinking the *U588* with *Wetaskiwin*. Until May 1944, she performed continuous convoy escort duty. She was present on D-Day. In October 1944, her anchors dragged during a storm in Iceland and she was wrecked on Videy Island near Reykjavik. A local resident bought her hull in 1945 and refloated it, but she was later broken up.

On September 1, 1939, Canada's naval fleet consisted of two Skeena Class destroyers, two training vessels, four Fraser Class destroyers and four mine-sweeping trawlers. Scattered across the nation were 312 officers and 3,292 men of the other ranks in the RCN, RCNR and RCNVR who were reasonably well trained and ready to go to war.

Twelve ships and thirty-six hundred men weren't much of a base on which to build a fighting navy. Yet it was light years ahead of the country's naval strength at the outbreak of hostilities in 1914.

CH14 and *CH15* were Canadian members of the British "H" Class of submarine. Displacement 364 tons surface–434 tons submerged/Length 150.25 feet/Width 15.75 feet/Forward draft 12.3 feet/Main engine oil/Full speed 13 knots surface–11 knots submerged/Endurance 1,100 nautical miles/Armament four 18-inch torpedo tubes/Crew 20–22. (Maritime Museum of British Columbia)

◁ Submarine crew members getting some fresh air aft of the tower around the open engine-room hatch.
(Maritime Museum of British Columbia)

▷ Crewman, *CH15*. (Maritime Command Museum)

▽ *CH15*, Bermuda 1922.
(Canadian Forces photograph/E-44274)

Sub CH15 1922

Above: HMCS *Saguenay*, first of name. As a River Class destroyer, her specifications were the same as *Skeena's*. (Canadian Forces photograph/CN-3068)

Right: HMCS *Skeena*, River Class destroyer. Displacement 1,337 tons/ Length 320 feet/Width 32 feet, 6 inches/Forward draft 11 feet/Main engines Parsons geared turbines/Full speed 31.5 knots/Endurance 3,450 nautical miles at 15 knots/Armament four 4.7-inch guns, eight 21-inch torpedo tubes and other lighter weapons. (National Maritime Museum/CTU2)

Left: HMCS *Skidegate*, a typical training vessel built in Vancouver in 1927. (Canadian Forces photograph/E-48)

HMCS *Thiepval*: Her trip around the world.

Thiepval was launched at Kingston, Ontario, in 1917 for the Department of Marine and Fisheries as a patrol vessel. Commissioned in the RCN in 1923 for west coast service, she was detailed to cross the Pacific to Hakodale, Japan, depositing fuel and oil supply dumps for the "around-the-world" flight of Major Stuart MacLaren. She salvaged what remained of MacLaren's aircraft after it was wrecked at Nikolski, Russia, on August 3, 1924. *Thiepval* was herself wrecked on an uncharted rock in Barkley Sound, B.C., in February 1930.

Above: HMCS *Thiepval* in Hakodale harbour, Japan.

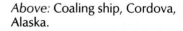

Left: Enjoying the old sucker after a day's work.

Above: Coaling ship, Cordova, Alaska.

Above: Men and women coaling *Thiepval* in Hakodale, Japan.

Lieuil Beech, Captain of *Thiepval*, in Japanese dress.

Pet on board HMCS *Thiepval*.

HMCS *Venture I*, commissioned in June 1937, Auxiliary Class schooner. Displacement 250 tons/Length 146 feet/Width 27 feet/Forward draft 14 feet/Sails 1,200 sq. ft./Main engine diesel/Armament two 3-pounder guns. (Canadian Forces photograph/0-781-2)

King George VI and Queen Elizabeth in Halifax, August 1939.
(Photo courtesy F. Chambers)

WORLD WAR II

Between the outbreak of war in 1939 and the conclusion of hostilities on board the U.S. battleship *Missouri* in Tokyo Bay on September 2, 1945, Canada changed from a "five trawler navy" to the third largest in the world. Its expansion was breathtaking in scope.

The fall of France in 1940 presented the British with such a serious problem that the Canadian government placed its entire navy at Britain's disposal. As a result of this act, the RCN was looked upon as part of the "negotiable assets" England had when dealing with the United States for areas of strategic responsibility.

When the Atlantic was divided by the Great Powers into these zones of strategic responsibility in September 1941, the United States took control of the western Atlantic using the RCN as a subordinate command of the American Navy. Reluctantly, Canada accepted this position because of her commitment to the mother country; she had a moral obligation to insure Britain's survival.

After the Japanese attack on Pearl Harbor in December 1942, the Americans were forced to withdraw most of their capital ships from Atlantic waters for use in the Pacific against the Japanese Navy. Canada suddenly found herself in the position of supplying nearly half of the Atlantic convoy escort protection, yet with no strategic control over the direction of her own growing navy. Absurdly, during the first half of the war Canada could only speak to the Americans through the British Admiralty Delegation in Washington! As the RCN struggled for autonomy it drifted naturally towards U.S Navy rather than Royal Navy influences.

But Atlantic convoy duties were only one part of the RCN's wartime role. Canadian warships sailed the "Murmansk Run" delivering life-saving convoys to Russia; they bombarded the Normandy coasts and took part in the D-Day invasion; they rescued refugees and were responsible for the sinking of twenty-six U-boats and two Italian submarines, seventeen through their own efforts. They were assisted in the destruction of the remainder by aircraft or warships of the British and American navies.

Canadian ships in increasing numbers became a familiar sight on the regular convoy route between Newfoundland and Ireland— the "Derry–Newfie run" as it was called by bittersweet romantics—especially ships of the "Barber Pole Brigade." The original members of this brigade were *Saguenay*, *Skeena*, *Sackville*, *Agassiz* and *Wetaskiwin*. Its name resulted from a discussion between two RCN lieutenants seeking distinctive markings for identifying their ships of the Fifth Escort Group. They settled on a band of red and white stripes painted slantwise on their ships' funnels. All of the group managed to survive their long, weary wartime service, with the exception of *Skeena*, which was wrecked off Iceland in 1944.

By war's end Canada's navy had grown to an astonishing 775 ships and 107,000 men and women, a remarkable accomplishment for a country with a population of only 10 million. However, this huge expansion of personnel created enormous problems. Only one person in thirty was properly trained, and to fill the new ships amateur weekend sailors, speedboat enthusiasts or anyone who had the slightest acquaintance with water craft were pressed into service.

Young lads with a few hours' experience in a 10-foot dinghy at their local sailing club suddenly found themselves as junior officers on board warships. Yet because Britain's position was so critical, Canada had no choice but to send raw recruits to sea to learn from the mistakes they made on the job. England's survival depended on the convoys. The British Admiralty decided that inexperienced convoy escorts and personnel were better than none at all.

However, both Britain and the United States remained critical of the amateurs that Canada had sent out to fight the war at sea. These young men endured dreadful hardships, uncertainty and boredom mixed with the acid taste of fear. Many of them never returned and only the restless waves mark their burial places. But their courage, strength and devotion to duty against frightening and, at times, nearly impossible odds will remain forever a source of pride to Canada. Theirs were the unsinkable Hearts of Oak.

Twenty-nine ships of the RCN were lost to enemy action or foundered at sea in stormy weather. Of the 106,522 men and women who served during World War II, 2,204 gave their lives; 319 were wounded in action.

HMCS Fraser	Destroyer	Sank	25/6/40	In Bay of Biscay after a collision with HMS Calcutta.
HMCS Bras d'Or	Aux. M/S		19/10/40	Foundered in Gulf of St. Lawrence.
HMCS Margaree	Destroyer		22/10/40	Collision with M/V Port Fairy in the North Atlantic.
HMCS Otter	A/S Yacht		26/3/41	Fire off Halifax.
HMCS Levis	Corvette		19/9/41	Torpedoed in North Atlantic.
HMCS Windflower	Corvette		7/12/41	Collision with SS Zypenberg in the North Atlantic.
HMCS Spikenard	Corvette		10/2/42	Torpedoed in North Atlantic.
HMCS Raccoon	A/S		7/9/42	Probably torpedoed in Gulf of St. Lawrence. Lost with all hands.
HMCS Charlottetown	Corvette		11/9/42	Torpedoed in Gulf of St. Lawrence.
HMCS Ottawa	Destroyer		13/9/42	Torpedoed in North Atlantic.
HMCS Louisburg	Corvette		6/2/43	Aerial torpedo in Mediterranean.
HMCS Weyburn	Corvette		22/2/43	Entrance to Straits of Gibraltar. Presumably mine or U-boat.
HMCS Athabaskan	Destroyer		29/4/44	Gunfire and torpedoed, English Channel.
HMCS Valleyfield	Frigate		7/5/44	Torpedoed off Cape Race.

Seven RCN motor torpedo boats were lost on D-Day in the English Channel.

HMCS Regina	Corvette	8/8/44	Torpedoed or mined in South Bristol Channel.
HMCS Alberni	Corvette	21/8/44	Torpedoed or mined, English Channel.
HMCS Skeena	Destroyer	25/10/44	Dragged ashore off Reykjavik, Iceland.
HMCS Shawinigan	Corvette	24/11/44	Cabot Strait, lost to enemy action with all hands.
HMCS Clayoquot	Bangor M/S	24/12/44	Torpedoed off Halifax.
HMCS Trentonian	Corvette	22/2/45	Torpedoed off Falmouth.
HMCS Guysborough	Bangor M/S	17/3/45	Torpedoed off Bay of Biscay.
HMCS Esquimalt	Bangor M/S	16/4/45	Torpedoed at Halifax Approaches.

HMCS *Bras d'Or*, auxiliary
minesweeper, lost in the
Gulf of St. Lawrence, 1940.

HMCS *Cougar*, one of sixteen private yachts purchased mainly from American owners for the RCN in 1940–41. Once the new corvettes became available during the summer of 1941, these ships were gradually transferred into training vessels and guardships.
(Canadian Forces photograph/E-11)

HMCS *Venosta*, auxiliary minesweeper.
(Canadian Forces photograph)

HMCS *Fundy*, a modified Basset Class minesweeper. Displacement 692 tons/Length 162 feet, 7 inches/Width 27 feet, 7 inches/Forward draft 10 feet/Main engine steam reciprocating (coal)/Full speed 12.5 knots/Armament one 4-inch gun, other weapons and minesweeping gear.
(Maritime Command Museum)

HMCS *Prince David*, one of three Armed Merchant cruisers in the RCN. The three—*Prince Henry* and *Prince Robert* were the other two—were luxury liners purchased from Canada Steamships and converted into warships early in 1940. *Prince David* was later converted into a landing ship for infantry and took part in the Normandy invasion. Displacement 6,000 tons/Length 385 feet/Full speed 22 knots/Endurance 3,600 nautical miles. (Canadian Forces photograph/E-36179)

Minelayer, Halifax.
(Parks Canada)

◁ HMCS *Thunder*, Bangor Class mine-sweeper. These oil-burning mine-sweepers—48 in all—became the backbone of the navy's minesweeping fleet. Sixteen assisted in sweeping the approaches for the fleet on D-Day and later cleared German mines from the English Channel. Displacement 672 tons/Length 180 feet/Width 28 feet/Forward draft between 9 and 10 feet/Full speed 16 knots/Endurance 2,950 nautical miles at 11.5 knots/Armament one 3-inch gun, one 12-pounder or 4-inch AA gun and other light weapons and minesweeping gear.
(Canadian Forces photograph/HS-0343-35)

HMCS *Cranbrook*, patrol vessel.
(Canadian Forces photograph/CN-3985)

HMCS *Magdalen*, one of eight Western Isles Class anti-submarine trawlers. Displacement 530 tons/Length 164 feet/Armament one 12-pounder and three 20-mm guns/Crew 40.
(Canadian Forces photograph/0-15170)

HMCS *Sault Ste. Marie*, one of 12 Algerine Class minesweepers. *Sault Ste. Marie* was the first of the class to join the RCN, on June 24, 1943. Displacement 990 tons/Length 225 feet/Width 35 feet/Forward draft 10 feet/Full speed 16 knots/Endurance 4,500 nautical miles at 11.5 knots/Armament one 4-inch gun and other smaller weapons.
(Canadian Forces photograph/E-11826)
▽

Merchant ships lie safely at anchor in Bedford Basin, waiting to form into a convoy. In the background are Dartmouth to the left and Halifax to the right.

△ HMCS *Ville de Quebec.* (Canadian Forces photograph/L-3126)   ▽ HMCS *Saskatoon.* (Photo courtesy Graham McBride)

△ HMCS *St. Thomas.*

▽ HMCS *Wetaskiwin.* (Canadian Forces photograph/E-153)

HMCS *Shediac*, one of the early Flower Class corvettes built for the navy at the beginning of the war. Over 100 of these small anti-submarine escorts were built in Canada; throughout the war they provided invaluable service on the North Atlantic convoy runs. Displacement 950 tons/Length 205 feet/Width 33 feet/Forward draft 8 feet, 3 inches/Full speed 16 knots/ Endurance 3,450 nautical miles at 12 knots/Armament one 4-inch gun, one 2-pounder, two 20-mm guns, hedge-hog and minesweeping gear. (Canadian Forces photograph/0-78-106)

Bottom left: HMCS *Smiths Falls* held the distinction of being the last corvette to enter the service during World War II. She was commissioned at Kingston on November 28, 1944, and had time to make three convoy crossings before the war ended. (Canadian Forces photograph/S-3210)

Below: HMCS *Trentonian*, one of the modified corvette designs built later in the war. Launched on September 1, 1943, it had twice the range of earlier models (Canadian Forces photograph/ PA-110924)

Ship's company, HMCS *Shediac*. (Photo courtesy Douglas Vincent)

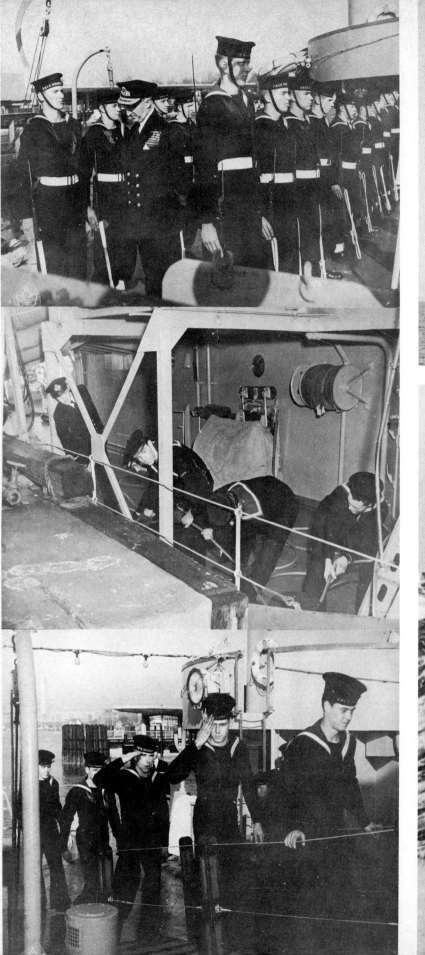

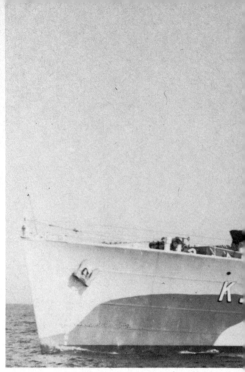

HMCS *Swansea*, one of seventy River Class frigates operated by the RCN during World War II. These were a specially designed escort vessel; larger than corvettes and much faster, they were closer to destroyers in their fire power yet much cheaper to build. They were the perfect answer to the U-boat menace. Displacement 2,000 tons/Length 301 feet/Full speed 20 knots/Armament two 4-inch guns, six 40-mm Bofors, two anti-submarine mortar mountings. (Canadian Forces photograph/E-5729)

At left: Inspection aboard.
(Canadian Forces photograph/HS-17268)

Crewmen at work.
(Canadian Forces photograph/HS-17272)

Crewmen going ashore.
(Canadian Forces photograph/HS-17269)

Overleaf: HMCS *Swansea.* ▷

Left: HMCS *Skeena* in Bermuda, 1937. In the background are *Saguenay* and *St. Laurent.* All were River Class destroyers.
(Maritime Command Museum)

Right: HMCS *Skeena* aground in Iceland, October 1944.
(Canadian Forces photograph/HS-1842)

Below: HMCS *St. Laurent.*

Overleaf: Ship's company, HMCS *St. Laurent.*
(Photo courtesy Commander Stephens) ▷

△ HMCS *Victoriaville.* (Canadian Forces photograph/DNS-25566)

△ HMCS *Waskesui.* (Canadian Forces photograph/HN-392)   ▽ HMCS *Halifax.* (Canadian Forces photograph/CN-3607)

Above: HMCS *Wallaceburg*, an Algerine Class coastal escort vessel. One of the first of her class to be built by the RCN, she was employed on escort duties during World War II.
(Canadian Forces photograph/0-601-1)

Left: HMCS *Wallaceburg*. In the background, HMS *United, Upright, Unseen* and *Unruffled*. (Photo courtesy Graham McBride)

Below: HMCS *Stonetown*.
(Canadian Forces photograph/Z-1578-R)

Above: HMCS *Sioux*, one of two "V" Class destroyers in the RCN. Here it arrives in Halifax, winter 1943.

Right: Chief Petty Officers of *Algonquin*. (Photo courtesy Sam Short)

Below: Algonquin bridge on D-Day. On right is Lt. General Harry Crerar, Commander of First Canadian Army. (Photo courtesy Sam Short)

Oiling at sea—heaving hose aboard
destroyer in Atlantic Ocean.
(Public Archives of Canada/PA-116335, photograph by
"Moses")

Below: HMCS *Haida*.
(Canadian Forces photograph/BN-1444)

Above: U-210 dives for the last time after being rammed by HMCS *Assiniboine*, August 6, 1942.
(Maritime Command Museum)

Left: U-210 survivors are taken aboard HMCS *Assiniboine*.
(Maritime Command Museum)

Above right: HMCS *Bayfield*, Bangor Class minesweeper, with Commandos on afterdeck, 1944.
(Canadian Forces photograph/E-3355)

Below right: Members of the Royal Canadian Navy during the invasion and liberation of Greece, October 1944.
(Public Archives of Canada/PA-116338, photograph by Milne)

Overleaf: HMCS *Uganda*, the only Canadian naval vessel engaged in the war with Japan. Displacement 8,800 tons/Length 555 feet, 6 inches/Width 62 feet/Forward draft 20 feet/Full speed 30.25 knots/Endurance 10,000 nautical miles at 12 knots/Armament nine 6-inch guns and six 4-inch guns/Crew 730. (Canadian Forces photograph)
▷

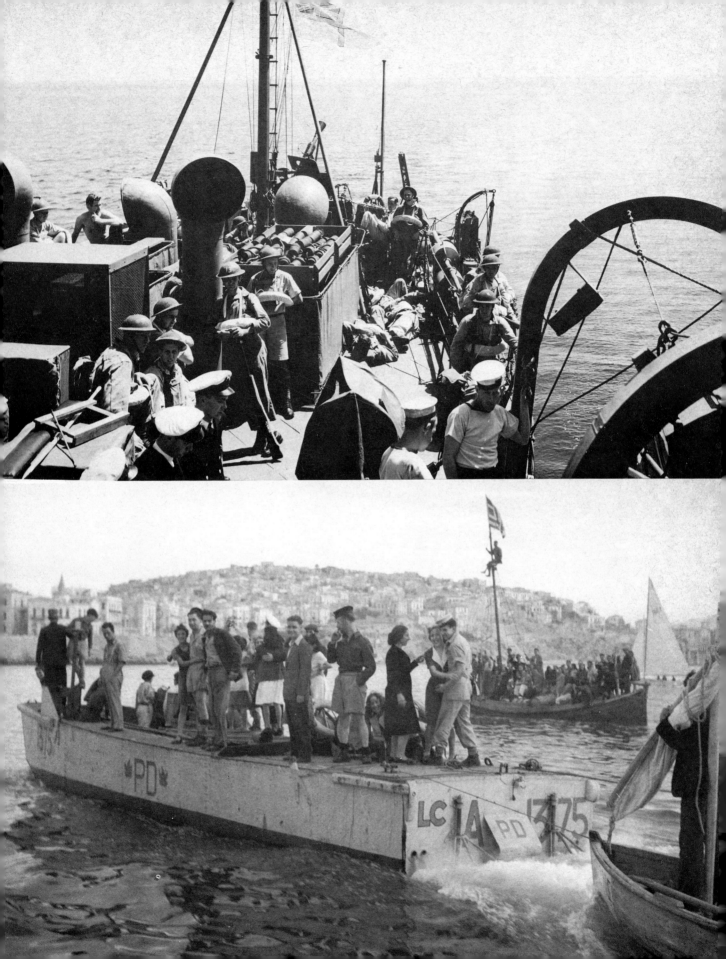

Above: HMCS *Columbia.*
(Canadian Forces photograph/0-4960)

Right: His Majesty King George VI
being piped aboard HMCS *Columbia,*
one of the Town Class destroyers,
from HMS *Kelly.*

Above: Churchill-Roosevelt meeting at Placentia Bay, Newfoundland, August 10, 1941. Here it was decided that the United States, still officially at peace, should share the task of protecting North Atlantic shipping. (Photo courtesy W.O. John Rainsford)

Left: Winston Churchill arrives on board HMCS *Assiniboine* at Placentia Bay for a brief visit with the Canadian sailors. (Public Archives of Canada/PA-140559)

Fairmile Anti-submarine Motor Launch. These were the little ships of the RCN. Between November 1941 and March 1944, sixty-seven were constructed. They were of unusual strength, endurance, and seaworthiness. They were also a dangerous craft in a fight because they used aviation 87 octane gasoline and exploded when hit in the tank by an incendiary bullet. Displacement 100 tons/Length 112 feet/Width 18 feet/ Full speed 24 knots/Endurance from 400 to 1,000 nautical miles/Armament three 20-mm Oerlikon guns, small arms and machine guns and 20 depth charges of 300 pounds each.

Top left: Halifax-based Fairmiles.

Bottom left: Fairmiles in Digby, Nova Scotia. (Photo courtesy Graham McBride)

Top right: Fairmile checking icebergs.

Bottom right: ML073 sending boarding party to submarine.
(Photo courtesy Cdr. LFL Hill, LCNR)

The Motor Torpedo Boat.
The RCN operated two types of MTB. Both were armed with a 6-pounder pom-pom gun and small automatics. On and after D-Day the MTBs served as escorts and helped guard the flanks of the invasion beaches and blockade enemy harbours.

The effects of freezing spray at sea.
(Canadian Forces photograph)

Above and below: HMCS *Brantford.*
(Canadian Forces photograph/NF-3587-2)

Right: HMCS *Shawinigan,* iced at anchor.
(Canadian Forces photograph/M-572)

THE KOREAN WAR

The Battles of the Atlantic had been won. Ships and men came home. Once more a sense of uncertainty enveloped the Naval Service. Personnel were demobilized, the fleet dismembered. People were tired of war. Old attitudes returned and the navy was again regarded as a burden to the taxpayer. Morale sank as those who were left retrenched and began planning for the future.

There had been morale problems during the war, but these had been suppressed by the necessity to get the job done. With the return of peace the problem of morale surfaced again. By 1948 matters were getting out of hand and a government commission was formed to examine the entire navy question. Its report noted the need for "Canadianization" of the service and for less dependence upon the traditions and iron-fisted discipline shown to men below decks of the Royal Navy. The Main–Guy Commission concluded that the RCN was out of step with the times.

The first problem arose from Canadian career naval officers serving with the Royal Navy, absorbing their attitudes and values. "Big Ship Time" often caused friction with RCNVR officers during the war. But with the RCNVR men gone, no buffer existed to soften the insensitivities of RCN career officers towards their subordinates. The friction between Royal Navy tradition and the new young recruits who reflected pride, independence and a spirit of Canadianism came as a shock to veteran officers who believed and followed the Royal Navy school of thought and discipline.

The navy recovered its morale with the Korean War. A U.N. Resolution condemned North Korea's invasion of South Korea, and a U.N. force of ships was dispatched to the war zone to stop the aggression. Several Canadian destroyers were included in the group.

No major naval engagements took place during the Korean War because the U.N. fleet controlled the coastal sea areas from the moment they arrived on station. The Canadian destroyers showed their versatility in naval blockade, gunfire support, anti-aircraft fire, defence of captured islands and checking "junks." Throughout, they were harassed by enemy batteries and moored or "drifter" mines.

HMCS *Haida*, *Athabaskan* and *Crusader* became members of the Korean "Trainbusters Club," a select group of American, Australian, Dutch and British destroyers. Trainbusting was the art of bombarding trains on rail lines travelling along the Korean coast. Gunners had to be fast and accurate to hit the trains between the tunnels where they hid between salvos. It became much like snap shooting in an arcade shooting gallery. HMCS *Crusader* topped the record among all the navies for the most trains destroyed.

Korea became mainly a gunnery war for the RCN. "Bombline" patrols provided gunfire support to Republic of Korea troops.

Targets were power stations, storage depots, railyards and covering fire during troop landings. The Canadian ships proved themselves with their speed, endurance and ability to close quickly on any target and deliver effective bombardment and firepower when it was needed.

Although a Naval Air Service was approved by the government in 1945 and the country had acquired a carrier—first the *Warrior*, later replaced by the *Magnificent*—for some reason operations were restricted to the carrier at sea.

During the Korean War, RCN naval aviators were anxious to see action with the *Magnificent*. But the proposal of placing the "Maggie" on the firing line in Korea was rejected on the grounds that the vessel's role was one of ASW—anti-submarine warfare— and not air-launched strikes. The pilots fumed at such illogical political reasoning. But since the navy was an arm of government, not the other way around, the decision remained unaltered.

HMCS *Magnificent*, a Light Fleet carrier lent by the Royal Navy to the RCN. It took part in numerous NATO and Canadian naval exercises throughout its career. Length 700 feet/Width 80 feet/Full speed 24.5 knots/Endurance 8,500 nautical miles at 20 knots/Armament anti-aircraft guns.
(Canadian Forces photograph/1416

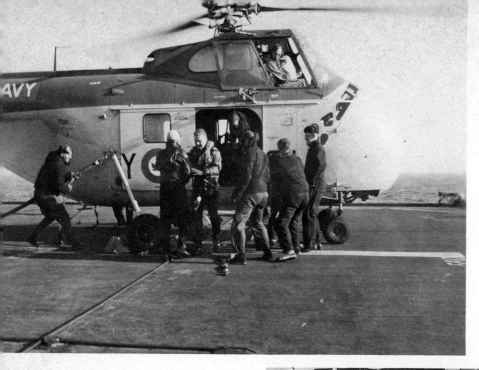

Helicopter on *Magnificent* flight deck after picking up the pilot from an aircraft that had ditched.
(Photo courtesy Cdr. Tate D.H.)

Aircrew attending briefing session on board HMCS *Magnificent*.
(Canadian Forces photograph/DNS-9973)

Installing extra fuel drop tank on Seafire aircraft.
(Canadian Forces photograph/DNS-9950)

Seafire ground looping on HMCS *Magnificent*.
(Photo courtesy Thomas Lynch)

Crewmen on deck, HMCS *Magnificent*.

Overleaf: Aircraft on board HMCS *Magnificent*. ▷

HMCS *Sioux*, one of the first three RCN destroyers to serve in Korea. She took part in the Inchon landings. Displacement 2,500 tons/Length 363 feet/Width 35 feet/Full speed 30.75 knots/Endurance 5,300 nautical miles at 15 knots/Armament four 4.7-inch guns and other smaller weapons. (Canadian Foces photograph/HS-67166)

Overleaf: HMCS *Athabaskan II*, Tribal Class destroyer. Displacement 1,990 tons/Length 377 feet/Width 37 feet, 6 inches/Forward draft 11 feet, 8 inches/Main engines Parsons geared turbines/Full speed 31.5 knots/Armament six 4.7-inch guns, four 21-inch guns, four 21-inch torpedoes. (Public Archives of Canada/PA-115446) ▷

TO THE PRESENT

After the 1950s Canada's destroyer-building program changed the look of the RCN. Instead of copying the Royal Navy, the RCN began developing and using its own ideas and technology for the first time. The first purely Canadian warship design was the St. Laurent Class. Innovations were made by the RCN for anti-submarine warfare, control systems, engines and hydrofoil designs.

The "Beartrap," a Canadian-developed helicopter hauldown device, enabled helicopters to land safely on ships at sea in stormy weather. This device led to the demise of the navy's aircraft carrier and fixed wing aircraft. A new generation of Canadian destroyer escorts was born. These were the helicopter destroyers carrying sub-hunting helicopters equipped with sonar listening devices capable of ranging wide areas of the ocean from a single ship at sea.

One of the consequences of these changes was that the navy's dream of operating a balanced fleet of large and small ships was over. The RCN's naval aviation branch received its death blow in 1969 with the retirement of the aircraft carrier *Bonaventure*. The RCN was to become strictly an escort navy of small ships operating in an anti-submarine role in conjunction with the larger naval forces provided by NATO members through STANAVFORLANT—NATO's Standing Naval Force, Atlantic. Canada's part in the force became embarrassingly small and, as time proved, ineffective for the defence of its own coasts and for providing submarine defence for the NATO navies.

These changes were the brainchild of Ottawa's Liberal government, who considered the DDH helicopter destroyers effective, politically acceptable and inexpensive to build and man. The government decided next on unification of the armed forces. The RCN would cease to exist as an individual service. Its symbol—the white ensign—would be folded away forever. Thus Canada, once a powerful maritime nation, allowed its navy to wither away through apathy and indifference until it became a joke to everyone but the proud men and women who served within its ranks. On February 1, 1968, the Royal Canadian Navy, as a legal entity, retired into the pages of history.

Yet, thanks to tireless dedication by our navy personnel and the election in 1984 of a new government in Ottawa, the future is beginning to look brighter. A new frigate program is now underway and there are plans to return naval personnel to their distinctive RCN uniforms and traditions. They deserve nothing less.

HMCS *St. Laurent II*, with "a bone in its teeth."

HMCS *Skeena I* and *II*.
(Canadian Forces photograph/E-40690)

With their light grey colour and smooth lines, three destroyer escorts of the Royal Canadian Navy—the *Skeena, Fraser* and *Margaree*—form an harmonious part of this waterfront scene at Saigon, South Vietnam. (National Defence photo/CR-317)

HMCS *St. Laurent II.*
(Canadian Forces photograph/HSPL-66-172-57)

Next spread: Ship's company,
HMCS *St. Laurent II.* ▷

HMCS *Assiniboine II*, one of the improved St. Laurent class destroyer escorts. These escorts were equipped with modern detection apparatus and weapons for the hunting and killing of submarines. Their streamlined hulls made them especially suited to combat icing conditions in the North Atlantic and to facilitate the washing down of nuclear fallout. Displacement 2,858 tons/Length 366 feet/Width 42 feet/ Full speed over 27 knots/Armament one twin 3-inch gun, triple-barrel anti-submarine mortars and homing torpedoes/Crew 210.
(Department of National Defence)

HMCS *Terra Nova*, one of the Restigouche Class destroyers built in reply to the development of newer, faster submarines. Displacement 2,390 tons/Length 371 feet/Width 42 feet/Full speed 28 knots/Armament two 3-inch anti-aircraft guns, 50-calibre machine guns, ASROC and IMK, 10 a/s mortars/Crew 241.
(Canadian Forces photograph)

Smoke from one salvo still swirls as anti-submarine mortars lower automatically to reload in the destroyer escort *Terra Nova*.
(Canadian Forces photograph/HS-75103-177)

The "Limbo" mortars fire projectiles weighing several hundred pounds in any direction and set to explode at any predetermined depth.
(Canadian Forces photograph/CN-3041)

HMCS *Terra Nova*.
(Canadian Forces photograph/HS68-1989)

The Canadian flag is lowered at sunset on board the HMCS *Terra Nova* in San Juan, Puerto Rico.
(Canadian Forces photograph/HS69-68/57)

HMCS *Nipigon II*, an Annapolis Class destroyer escort equipped with hangar and flight deck for operation of anti-submarine helicopters. It is also fitted with the Canadian variable depth sonar system. Displacement 2,858 tons/Length 371 feet/Width 42 feet/Forward draft 14 feet, 4 inches/Main engines geared turbines/Full speed 28 knots/Armament one twin 3-inch gun, triple-barrel ASW mortar, homing torpedoes/Crew 210.
(Canadian Forces photograph/SW72-417)

Above right: HMCS *Annapolis*.
(DND: IMOC 76-2352)

Below right: HRH The Prince of Wales—Lieutenant Charles Windsor—leaves *Annapolis* after a visit.

The fleet at anchor in Halifax's
Bedford Basin. (Maritime Command Museum)

Above: HMCS *Porte St. Jean*, one of five Gate Class trawlers built as fleet auxiliaries in 1951. In wartime they were to be used operating the gate mechanisms at entrances to harbours that were defended by submarine nets. They could also be used as coastal mine sweepers. Displacement 460 tons/Length 130 feet/Full speed 11 knots/Armament one 40-mm gun/Crew 23.
(Canadian Forces photograph/HS-65-909)

Left: HMCS *Trinity*, one of four new Bay Class minesweepers built in 1953. Displacement 412 tons/ Length 152 feet/Width 28 feet/ Sweeping speed 12 knots/Endurance 3,000 nautical miles at 12 knots.
(Canadian Forces photograph/HS-36853)

Below: Crewmen of HMCS *Trinity* with Spike, the ship's pet.
(Canadian Forces photograph/H-1833)

Right page: HMCS *Victoriaville*, a Prestonian Class frigate, followed by the *Inch Arran* and the *New Waterford*. (DNS-30094)

Above: HMCS *Ojibwa.*
(Canadian Forces photograph/HS66-523-108)

Right: HMCS *Onondaga.*
(Canadian Forces photograph/HS66-523-105)

Left: HMCS "O" Class submarines *Onondaga, Ojibwa* and *Okanagan*. (Canadian Forces photograph/HS79-1333)

Below: HMC submarines *Onondaga* (73) and *Ojibwa* (72) of the First Canadian Submarine Squadron tied up in HMC Dockyard, Halifax. (Canadian Forces photograph/HS67-2249)

Right: Five U.S. submarines are tied up in HMC Dockyard, Halifax, along with the Canadian submarine HMCS *Ojibwa* (72). (Canadian Forces photograph /HS67-2398)

HMCS *Bonaventure*, a modified Majestic Class aircraft carrier. Displacement 20,000 tons/Length 704 feet/Width 112 feet/Armament eight 3-inch guns for anti-aircraft defence and four 6-pounders for saluting/Crew 1,370. It carried 34 Banshee jet and piston driven Tracker aircraft.
(Canadian Forces photograph/HS-69-3061)

Above: HMCS *Bonaventure*.
(Canadian Forces photograph/BV68-1173)

An air force and an army pilot have been teamed with two navy anti-submarine systems operators to form the first fully integrated Tracker crew to fly from the aircraft carrier *Bonaventure*. (Canadian Forces photograph/ BV69-445)

Salute to *Bonaventure*'s final return as she passes the breakwater into Halifax harbour.
(Canadian Forces photograph/HS68-649)

Left: HMCS *Bonaventure* fires a 21-gun national salute as she leads a seven-ship Canadian naval task group into port at New Orleans.
(Canadian Forces photograph/BV68-372)

Flight deck of HMCS *Bonaventure*.
(Canadian Forces photograph/BN-509)

HMCS *Bonaventure* is given her final salute as she arrives in Halifax to end her last operational cruise.
(Canadian Forces photograph/HS69-3045)

Above: The scene at Falsane, Scotland, as Vickers Oceanics' *VOL L1* submersible and HMCS *Ojibwa* prepare for a sea floor rendezvous during which men will transfer from the submersible, via the mating skirt, into the Canadian submarine.

Left: Cdr. Brian Forbes, RN, Flotilla Escape, Rescue and Diving Officer—first man to transfer from Vickers Oceanics' *VOL L1* submersible into the Canadian submarine HMCS *Ojibwa*—hands a commemorative plaque to the submarine's commander, Lt. Cdr. Lloyd Barnes, as he emerges from the connecting escape tower.

Above: Units of the First
Canadian Minesweeping Squadron
proceed to sea in arrowhead
formation. Clockwise from the top
they are HMC ships *Quinte* (149),
Fundy (159), *Thunder* (161),
Chignecto (160), *Chaleur* (164) and
Resolute (154).
(Canadian Forces photograph/DNS-30932)

HMCS *Fundy III.*
(Canadian Forces photograph/HS-49813)

Above left: HMCS *Provider II*, a fleet supply vessel that carries supplies of oil, food, spares and helicopter parts for the navy's fleet. Displacement 22,700 tons/Length 551 feet/Width 76 feet/Forward draft 30 feet/Full speed 20 knots/ Crew 142.

Below left: "Now Hear This!" Bosn's pipe over the ship's intercom on board *Provider II*.
(Canadian Forces photograph)

Above right: HMCS *Preserver*.
(Canadian Forces photograph/RE70-1253)

Below right: Mother hen supply ship *Preserver* with two chickens at sea.

Canadian
warships
performed this
special close
formation fleet
exercise off the
coast of Puerto
Rico.
(Canadian Forces
photograph/BV68-476)

Left: HMCS *Athabaskan III*, one of four Iroquois Class destroyers. Displacement 3,551 tons/Length 398 feet/Width 50 feet/Forward draft 14 feet/Armament one 5-inch gun, one Limbo, homing torpedoes, two Sea Sparrow missiles, two Sea King helicopters/Crew 244.
(Canadian Forces photograph/SWC72-1682)

Below: HMCS *Huron*.

Overleaf: HMCS *Iroquois*. ▷

HMCS *Labrador*, commissioned in 1954, carried the most modern scientific equipment available at the time. When she was paid off in 1957, she was the only RCN ship ever to transit the Northwest Passage. (Canadian Forces photograph/1016)

Crewmen of HMCS *Labrador*.
(Canadian Forces photograph)

Above: HMCS *Quest*, Agor 172
oceanographic research vessel.
Built for acoustic hydrographic and
general oceanographic work, in
particular as related to anti-
submarine warfare. Displacement
2,130 tons/Length 253 feet/Width
42 feet/Forward draft 15.5 feet/Main
engines diesel electric/Full speed 16
knots/Endurance 10,000 nautical
miles at 12 knots/Crew 55.
(Defence Research Establishment Atlantic)

Below: HMCS *Endeavour*.

Queen Elizabeth, the Queen
Mother, hands over the new
Queen's colour for Maritime
Command in Halifax.
(Canadian Forces photograph/HSC79-2449-24)

HMCS *Sackville*, Agor 113 research
vessel. Originally launched in 1941,
this Flower Class corvette was
converted to a loop layer. Plans
were to restore her to original
corvette configuration in time for
the grand sail past celebrating the
75th anniversary of the RCN in 1985.
(Bedford Institute of Oceanography/26385)

HMCS *Sackville* on Atlantic patrol in
November 1942. (Department of National
Defence and the Maritime Command Museum)